GOLDILOCKS IN LATER LIFE

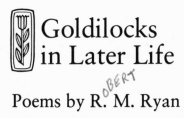

Goldilocks in Later Life

Poems by R. M. Ryan

Louisiana State University Press
Baton Rouge and London 1980

For my mother and in memory of my father

Copyright © 1980 by R. M. Ryan
All rights reserved
Manufactured in the United States of America

Designer: Patricia Douglas Crowder
Typeface: VIP Sabon
Typesetter: LSU Press
Printer: Thomson-Shore, Inc.
Binder: John Dekker & Sons, Inc.

Grateful acknowledgment is made to the editors of the
following publications in which some of these poems have
appeared: *Denver Quarterly, Intro #2, Poetry NOW,* and
Sackbut Review.

LIBRARY OF CONGRESS CATALOGING IN PUBLICATION DATA

Ryan, R   M
    Goldilocks in later life.
    I. Title.
PS3568.Y393G6   811'.5'4   79–21136
ISBN 0–8071–0679–8
ISBN 0–8071–0680–1 pbk.

CONTENTS

Goldilocks in Later Life

GOLDILOCKS IN LATER LIFE

Once she's left, she'll never see again
the pathway back nor come upon the place
where the door's unlatched and breakfast waits.
For her, the porridge will come to be
always too hot or cold,
and all the beds will make her restless.

From that day on, the three of them
will find the woods darker than before,
and Baby Bear, who wanted
more than anything
to grow up,
will finally get his wish,
though he won't forget
the strands of golden hair
or the scent of perfume on his sheets.

And we who tell the tale
sit awkwardly in the tiny chair
beside our children's beds
as we leave the bears waiting hand in hand
at the end of what happened long ago.
The children—who all too soon will learn
that the woods, the golden girl are gone,
that all the bears are dead—
sleep soundly and, for the moment,
live happily ever after.

WHAT THE TALES WERE TELLING US

They warned us all along
that granny might not be there
if we dallied in the woods too late,
that we might, though saved,
find ourselves among dwarfs
or end up listening to a fox
whose improbable advice
would turn out, later, to be true.

But we didn't hear.
As we wandered toward the house
we found but didn't want,
we grew so terrified
we didn't listen.
Inside the mirror
was a face changed beyond
what any kiss could do.

And even if whole ponds of frogs
get kingdoms ringed with gold,
the spell which kept us children
will not come back
unless the voice which sent us on our way
becomes our own
as we tell the other children setting out
you'll come upon a time but once.

PROMETHEUS MINOR

What the sun does
simply being there
you must do, over and over,
with a piece of flint,
two brittle sticks
on a windy plain
where rain is about to fall.

TO AESOP

The tortoise is older now. It's doubtful
if he could make it home without a pause.
The shepherd's boy is a congressman and says
he'll stamp corruption out. The fox owns a ladder.
He burps and seldom dreams of grapes.

                                    Old friend,
you worked hard to find the ant's success,
yet there's no moral in these later scenes
where the race is not so quick and never won
by those who know the rules but not the game.

And of your end, no word. Were you secreted off
by friends to some dark place where you babbled,
your clear wit turned at last to mindless banter,
or sent among the crippled old to beg
along Athenian streets? Perhaps you fell bleeding
to the gutter, beaten by thieves. And doubts,
persistent as flies on carrion, pursued you to the end.

DELPHI

Speaking in what, to me,
is an unknown tongue,
our guide lectures us in Greek.
The German lady I stand beside
translates, in broken English,
the content of some half-known myths.

My guidebook adds little else:
the pensions, the restaurants
that specialize in squid,
and a one-page history of 2000 years—
a tale of gods who didn't last
and of tourists, who did.

The Charioteer,
with his astonished eyes,
the reins that seem to quiver,
is silent,
looking perhaps beyond us all,
in horror, at where his horses go.
The wind flips through
my guidebook leaves
as if there is something
it can't quite find.

FROM THE HANDSOME PRINCE

She crossed my horizon like a giant.
In a symphony of jewels,
my slime turned gossamer

as I rose to her
with a rain intricate as lace.

While I forgot
how long I waited
ignored in warts,

I didn't notice
how tightly her saddle fit
or that I slept in sweat

as she rode away from me
toward something else to kiss.

BEAST FABLE

At the beginning of the tale,
the lazy boy is drowned by frogs.
The girl who didn't wash her face
is carried off by crows,
and the foxes wait
for those who wouldn't go to bed.

In the part told on television,
the chimpanzee is drinking beer
while a man walking through the wilderness
explains that the boa and the iguana
do exactly what they should
and nothing more.

But now the story grows
more difficult to understand.
Remembering the tribesmen masked
as elephants while they shoot
a kind of LSD
up each other's noses
is no longer funny, nor is their belief
that we are wild. Not now,
when all we hear from the spotless corridors
is a hum both useless and precise
as the ice machines and elevators
go predictably about their business.

It doesn't help to know
that little here is wild;
that the vitamins
are separated from the morphine;
that the faucets are marked
WATER, AIR, and DO NOT TOUCH;
that the cheap Parisian print
is clearly labeled PARIS.
Nothing—not the charts

where cancers are graphed like stocks—
will make the ending right.

We only know that the patient,
wasted until he looks like someone
who barely escaped the famine,
reminds us of geographies
we haven't mapped, animals
who teach no lessons.

Against the fresh white walls
the sack of blood
seems a dark uncertainty
as it empties toward
the wilderness inside.

The Man Who Wasn't
There Arrives

THE MAN WHO WASN'T THERE ARRIVES

My life has been a pretty dull affair,
spent in towns you didn't know were there.
My high school annual left my picture out,
and I began to put myself in doubt
when people said they'd seen me other days
walking briskly on the Champs Élysées
or throwing pennies in Niagara Falls.
"But no," they'd say, "it wasn't you at all.
He had a darker face, a finer nose . . .
something in the way he wore his clothes.
Still, I can't help but see him in your face."
They'd walk away, thinking of another place,
a man I've never known.

                              Someday, for a laugh,
I'll tell them "Yes, that was me you saw at Banff,
hooded face, looking thin and pale,
or in Kansas stomping through the wheat for quail.
Think . . . I took pictures of your accident;
I cleaned the sickroom for your dying aunt.
I've lived with you like leaves with fall;
you've heard me walk behind you down the hall.
And like the leaves, all my faces mean the same,
and they will someday bring you to my name.
Next time you'll know it's me that's come.
When I arrive, there'll be no place to run."

THE DISAPPEARANCE OF AMERICA

Think of all the towns that died, of Brilliant
gone; of Shakespeare, of Golden, even Bland,
where lives went on, like those of Madam Varnish
and her daughters or Hubert Love, who fought
a bear and won. Think about the coffin
M. C. Logan kept inside his store,
about the Ethel Silver Trumpet Band.
Think of Turkey Creek Jack Johnson now
or the blurred girl who moved in the photograph
of the Chance City July the Fourth parade
as you go home, hardly noticing
the cars that pass and are not seen again.

AND WHO IS YOUR PARTNER FOR THIS EVENING'S DANCE?

Hey, this sure is fun
and, wow, let's go

around and around
until the sofa blurs,

the cupboard smears,
the rose becomes a purple slash.

O that this could last
forever

you wish
until you learn

it does.

NO HELP

They will never help, these stars;
nor will the peculiar shade of green
the moonlight through the curtains
leaves upon the untouched bed.
The whiskey bottle becomes its empty self.

Tomorrow won't be better.
Whatever sermons were hidden in the stones
are wearing down to sand.
The light is broken by the boughs,
and the birds grow silent at our approach.

MARCH REQUEST

Let the statue of
Winged Victory Over Ignorance
decay without a word.

Let the images collapse
to bushes, trees, and sky.
They at least remain.

Let the wind blow hard—
a great scouring,
a truth too hard to tell.

A WARNING FROM THE NOVELIST

You won't be he or she or they.
A good thing too,

the way this book subverts
your famous wish

for immortality.
How the people disappear!

Think of poor old Mumbles.
He only got one line.

Keep yourself away.
The lives in here

are made up of sentences,
and they are always carried out.

GRIEF

Had eggs for breakfast. Listened awhile to Mozart.
Mrs. Gottfried died. To bed at ten.
The sky turned oddly bright—and over and over:
Eggs and Mozart. Mrs. Gottfried. Sky.

The hand that shaped these lines. The hand that
    holds them.
Not quite touching. Not quite making sense.
Details turning to some final form.
Eggs and Mozart. Mrs. Gottfried. Sky.

WHAT THE MASTER SAID

Coming to this place
takes years.

The way is hard
on purpose

so you'll believe
that the journey from Etruria

must be undertaken,
that only the Tsahi

will keep the dark
from weighting down your shoes.

But now that you've come,
I've forgotten

why I led you on
or what it was, if anything,

I'd show you.
In fact,

I seldom think of you,
except to wonder if

you sit, like me,
in your underwear

staring at a photograph,
its colors no longer true,

of one who thought
that he'd arrive

where no one else has been.

KILLING THE FATHERS

Yes, it's awful
and of course

I understand exactly
what you're doing

with that bloody heart,
that xylophone of ribs.

You're getting it all—
the cancer, the ulcer,

the shattered brains as well.
See, you have it

in those hands,
in those hands you've seen before.

A KIND OF AFRICA

The jungle is darker than you supposed.
It's more than just the trees.
You expected them.
Even the parrot flying backward
is distant and thus improbable.

The trees who remind you of your relatives,
the sun slivered like the piece of glass
you once saw winking in the trash
are not.

The one who takes care of this
you will find
solitary in a clearing.
Expecting you, he'll be wearing ornaments
which resemble dreams.

You'll want to trade for them.

Keep this in mind while you wait,
face-to-face with shrunken heads.
Hanging from his door,
they see, if anything at all,
a day dwindled to their eyes.

A QUIZ ON THE SEASONS

This year, do you look more closely as
the frost upon your windowpane
designs what almost look like ferns
becoming fossils on your view?

This spring, beneath the churning gray,
when the streets are drowned, the sewers full,
and the scene turns bleary through the glass,
do you wonder where Atlantis is?

PROGRAM NOTES

The Vivace
beginning this symphony
is among the shortest ever written.
The musicians,
in their serious clothes,
will grimace as they finish up
its difficult
but minor variations.

Then, the Diminuendo,
quite unlike the major parts;
and you won't mistake
its piccolos
for the timpani and bass
introducing,
with bits of children's songs,
the sounding of the signature
for the final Appassionata.

The orchestra will stop
and momentarily we'll wait
together in anticipation
before we go plunging back,
alone, into the major theme
the one that long ago appeared
the one we can't forget,
as suddenly, and far too soon,
it will be coming to an end.

A Place Altogether Elsewhere

AFTER THE WORST IS KNOWN

Now is not the time
for the tall words
in their startling clothes.

No more will be said
of what the gnats mean
gathering

to disappear.
The woods are closed,
the season of allegory

done. Instead
rattle off your list
of where you'll go

and what you'll do
as if you really will
survive.

That much they'll understand,
the ones
who go on planning

new ways to exchange
fives for ones
and ones for fives

while at night
keep meeting
what isn't true—

the man in feathers
bowed down by gravity
reading by a fire

in the Book of Hieroglyphs
of shapes like water
in words like air.

SEEING THE MUMMY

Before he died, did he confess
that lotus made his breath taste sour,
that lapis couldn't bribe the hours
which dragged him into nothingness,
that golden masks were not his skin?
Are these thoughts resined in his head?
Then why this work to guard the grin
of a man who's kept because he's dead?

Too bad he didn't die unknown,
go before he planned to die,
like one who felt the sudden stone
or found mist instead of air
while he ran dizzily up the stairs.
Mauve dots ballooning in his eyes.
Death is here, a complete surprise.

THE PROFESSOR LOST IN THE DICTIONARY

Under his little light
he is tired.
The words do not make
sense.

"For example,"
he says bravely to the dark,
"the origin of *genius* is about
both begetting and being born.
It refers, my god, to everyone,
including, in French, civil engineers."

"Who are these people?"
he demands to know,
not listening to a darker voice,
which absorbs more light,
sing Diddy Wah Diddy
while the muddy waters flow.

A SPELLING LESSON

At first it is a matter of
Getting the letters in a row
To mean and in meaning so
To mean what you were thinking of.

If, for example, you say snow,
Then snow should be all your reader sees.
Not the trees it lies on nor the skies
From which it falls as if to disguise

All the world that lies below.
No, the snow should be merely snow,
Though snow beneath the sun's bright spell,
Is water and later air as well.

Confusing? They surely are to me,
These variant abracadabras hurled
To spell the various shifting world,
Though a famous magician once said to me

The trick is simply what you see.

SANTA REPLIES

When I was your version,
you believed.

Now I bring what you deserve.
If you buy gifts

that are really for yourself,
the town merely looks like gingerbread.

It eats you up
while you shovel out

those rigid pathways to your door.
And no one comes

except me.

I'll find you out
no matter how you hide behind

those decorations of yours.
I won't be playing Santa,

though I'll be the hugest red
you've ever felt.

I hope you can survive
this attack of heart,

so I bring another gift.
You must unwrap yourself

by imagining
how to sit

forever,
the world's best wishes on your knee.

Your fat, while it won't be real,
will have a meaning and a name.

You'll stay warm where it is always winter
as you make yourself to give away

radiant in this northern light.

YOU'VE HEARD THIS ONE BEFORE

When the man beside you at the bar
begins speaking in a way
you no longer understand,
you'll know the story that he tells
was here before he thought of it or you

or of how Martin and LaTour
met tribesmen counting up their furs
as they sang of how the Phoenicians came
while the man whose entire history's lost
tells this to the one he sits beside

in a place altogether elsewhere
as the laughter and the footfalls
fade and the wind goes round
until a voice strangely like your own
says Excuse me, I didn't hear.

THE WELSH SHEPHERD TO THE SCHOLAR

All those *l*'s are there on purpose
and will not fit your tongue
unless you give in to them.

Sounds of obedience and pain,
our few vowels
will be easier for you.

If you stay around,
the goats won't smell so bad
as you come to understand

what all those castles
surviving in their distance
mean.

LOOKING AT THE FAMILY PHOTOGRAPHS
for my grandmother on her 90th birthday

i

Although we might imagine
Snoda, Amaziah, and the rest
coming by wagons from their farms
in their new suits and dresses
stiff as saddle leather
when they left, for one brief day,
their enormous work to stay alive,
their photographs show nothing
of how they lived but Bibles.
What might have been
one of those dappled Saturdays in June
is as absent as whiskey.

With rigid eyes
they stare like accusations
at the snapshots surrounding them
until the future seems
a prophecy come true.
Our summers at the lake,
the skiing trips,
the new convertible—   **2089875**
all the colors of our lives
are fading to the earth
most of them are buried in.

ii

Out of all these people,
just one survives
and can explain the photograph
taken that summer of '29
of her closest relatives
while they stood on the veranda
of the house in Mount Ayr, Iowa,
as if expecting us.

They could not imagine,
she tells us now,
themselves not here,
not think of Edgar dead
that winter of influenza,
Uncle Spenser broke
in Tallahassee, Florida,
the pigtailed little girl
unable, at the end, to dress herself.

There, the future brings only dinner
and, later, naps
and games of hide and seek
in that moment when they paused forever,
on that afternoon
where night will never come.

PLAYING THE GAMES

In Monopoly
our wooden representatives
landed on their fortunes
until each other's property
cost one of us too much.

We left off Scrabble
when messages kept turning up.
Clue was worse,
all those accusations
in the bedroom and the hall.

So having thrown away
our set of Bridge for Honeymoons,
we sit together and alone,
tallying up one final hand
of Solitaire for Two.

FLOWERS ON OUR WEDDING ANNIVERSARY
for Juli

Do they remind you of the magnolia tree
we sat beneath, listening to the organ fugue?
Are they for the lies about forever
magnolia blooms and Johann Sebastian Bach
somehow managed to inspire? At times,
I want to reach inside my memory
and drag, like our children, those lovers out
to the rusted toys I've found beneath the snow
and scold them with another kind of lie
about preserving everything that's dear.
And yet I know that all our care has kept
our bridal china unbroken but untouched.
Let them go. The wind assaults those blooms
as the last chord shatters into silence.

MY FORMER MUSE

Nothing's been the same since that afternoon
I met her in the park and she let me feel
inside her blouse. She bit my ear and moaned,
"It's never happened quite this fast before."
She also told me "Wait" and pointed at
the huge and gargoyled house across the street.
"My husband's dying. Wait and get it all:
the house, the summer place in Maine, and me."

That was years ago. I still drop by with gifts,
even though she married someone else,
who now, she whispers, "won't outlast the month."
She lets me kiss her cheek, smooths down her skirt,
and stands beside the window looking out
toward the park, at someone I can't see.

THE DISCOVERY OF A COUNTRY WHERE
FICTION THRIVES *for Wallace Stevens*

It was not, as I'd expected, like Florida
or the South of France or even Connecticut.
Instead of a linen suit, a tie from Brooks,
I found myself in Big Mac overalls
as I walked where litter blew and addicts stared
at the insides of their eyes, which, like the windows
of the shops I passed, were empty and opaque.

The train I boarded had the crusty smell
of after shave and farts, but it headed south.
So eating apples with the taste of chalk,
I rode through a landscape like a parking lot
until I arrived to the sound of an oompah band
and, in a voice like that of Donald Duck's,
a matron singing "Our Boy's Come Home at Last."

AN ATTEMPTED EXPLANATION OF THE SUN

He waited for the world to speak
that old transfiguring of the sun
which turned a color no one's named
to the ruddy clay beside the trees,
to the iridescent and moonlit hedge.

While they were there, the words were not.
The image could not be written yet,
transfiguring silence into speech
the ruddy iridescent scene,
the one and many-colored sun.

MAN CRYING ON THE DECK

Enough of all our little lives. Enough
of what we didn't mean to be but are.
Enough. It's morning once again. The sun,
while not as bright as the day we started off
when good wishes like confetti flew,
manages to shine, and the winds are strong.
Although the maps are vague about the reefs,
let's set another course, decide to go
if only because the going makes us move.
The future, which years from now, will seem a
    chapter
from a book that no one reads, is empty,
waiting for us to fill its story in.
Let's find an ending that hasn't chosen us.

The Light Whose Name
Is Splendor

WHAT TO SAY

Words? Foolishness, I know,
against the darkness coming on,
but then, what really works? So talk,
if only some private thought of elves
or if you think that way, talk facts.
Speak of amperes or chromosomes
or the molecules of hydrogen.
Soon, if your talk is right, it turns
into a kind of charm. *Therefores*
changing into abracadabra
against the brute descent of sun.
Maybe this time the dark will brighten
almost as if it noticed us.

A LOVE POEM
for Carol

When I kiss you,
I taste another earth,
a soil deep loamed and fertile
where gypsies spoke a tongue
as distant from us as birds
and the wheat ripened like a consequence
and the master and the maiden walked
without underwear beneath their felt
in *belles heures* inscribed in gold
and the monk paddling on the castle lake
spoke Greek to a world flat as paper
and the man who thinks all this
speaks in colors and a shape or two
in a world deep beyond belief
and deepening like
the many speeches of the earth.

THE SOLUTION

Are you beginning to see?
It's as clear as water,
around you from the start.

Didn't you notice
how the killer ran across your porch?
Those cries were not just birds.

The heavy thump
was more than just a tremor
in your heart.

The shape behind you in the mirror,
the one you almost
recognized—

a figment
of whose imagination?

Be careful. Your detective
should ignore your evidence.
Pay him to.

Make sure the handcuffs
are shaped for someone else
and even

if the real culprit's
caught,
remember that Justice

finally is blind:
the truest mysteries

are never solved.

VISIONS OF ST. LOUIS
Site of the 1904 World's Fair

St. Louis knew.
His statue reminds us
that grace endures,

even though our climate
has left stains below his eyes
like tears at how the fair

has turned into a slum,
the bricks sinking,
the roads breaking up

as if they had no place to go
but away
from the squalor

our intentions have become.
And yet the meaning
of the ordinary earth

glowed
like Noah's rainbow
around the host

of the golden dead
who gathered here to meet me
one winter night.

But I was afraid,
choosing to stay
among the awfulness

of a world where, X-rated,
Alice in Wonderland
plays with *Flesh Gordon*.

I trusted what is ugly,
and I pay. In a dream,
the ancient boat, which smells of fear,

sets out, as I knew it would,
toward that uncertain, other shore
where those I know

wait, each in his appointed place,
to counsel and to curse me
with tales of what might have been.

All around,
the great, entangling dark
strangles every light.

That others walked this way before
will be of little help
as lost, uncertain,

I, in walking, find
what joy there is
in moving one foot, then another

through my time
and all the time which came before.
St. Louis, now mute

in my disbelief,
will tell me nothing
of what he knows.

I am alone
with only the song
Alceste sang

to speak with death:
Divinités du Styx,
Divinités du Styx

as I try to raise myself
from the death entombed
in every limb.

And song is all I have.
Though my air diminish every day,
Divinités du Styx.

Hear, O hear,
on all the earth I have,
as I sing,

to make the darkness go away,
Divinités du Styx.
And the dead, the dead are listening.

Yes! From a time outside of memory,
on the earth, which in changing,
doesn't change,

on the mounds
the Cahokia built,
on the seas

the Vikings sailed,
on all the times,
the song—O yes—returns.

Do you hear?
The wind from Smyrna has it;
the wind across Ceylon

is blowing here
across the dead which make our earth.
The wind which stirred their hair

is stirring ours.
The deep grass
begins to shudder,

and I begin to hope
that the light whose name is splendor
will shine on me again.

STAGES
for Jim Comfort, killed by accident

No, not here, where the lights are going down,
but there, in the made-up bright, where all is set,
Fortunatas, who knows ahead of time
which sword will fall, keeps away from us
until, the final curtain coming down,
he offers his regards to everyone.
Ourselves again, about to talk, we step
into the lobby's sudden noise and out

toward the street's ill-lit uncertainties.
One couple almost stumbles from the curb
as a headline comes tearing through the wind,
flattening on signs for a close-out sale.
We go home exhausted and sleep through dawn,
the morning broken crimson on the ground.

FALL LETTER TO A FRIEND

With our trees and our weather
we survive, holding our own against
the gaudy descent of leaves
whose promise of apocalypse leads
each year to winter.
We, too, settle

but not, thank God, so fast
that we'll miss the spring
or what our children do
scattering through the leaves
that become the decay
which brings the living forth.

The Magical Daughter

Once upon a time—and a long, long time ago it was—there lived a little girl.

If you had met her, you wouldn't see anything special about this little girl. She seemed ordinary as could be. In fact, you might not have seen her at all, hidden as she often was among the flowers in the garden behind her parents' cottage or sitting in the farthest corner of her room behind the dolls she played with.

She spoke with the flowers and taught her dolls to dance. But people—even her parents—were in a world apart from her. Oh, she smiled at them and sometimes, if prodded, spoke, but mostly she sat by herself and sang a little tune that could only be heard if you kneeled down near where she sat among the flowers or the dolls. And if you came too close, she would smile distantly at you and stop her song.

"My daughter doesn't love me," her mother said.

"My daughter won't bring my slippers after dinner," her father said.

They were both sad because their daughter seemed to ignore them.

The mother had a chest her mother had given her. It was filled with all kinds of things: handkerchiefs and hats, dresses and dolls, lace and linens, recipes and romantic perfumes—all the treasures all the mothers in the family had wanted to give their daughters.

The father wanted to show his daughter what he had done to their land. He wanted her to see the hedge his father had planted on the soil his father's father had taken care of. Once the hedge had been tiny and delicate, like the little girl, but it had grown large and full, as would she.

But the daughter seldom came to them. She ignored the hedge her father loved and wouldn't go with her mother to the dark attic where the chest was kept.

She sat by herself and smiled and sang.

Some nights, long after the little girl was in bed and dreams, her parents sat together by the fire and talked over what they might do to make their daughter love them.

Often they just sighed and hoped that she would someday come to them.

One night—all those many years ago in that little cottage with the hedge—they fell asleep on the couch before the fire.

As they slept, their heads came together, and their hands slowly joined. The fire began to flicker and almost died.

Then it suddenly flared again and in its flaming formed a kind of shape that the parents, who were sleeping very soundly, didn't see.

The shape became clearer and clearer and soon took the form of a lovely woman who resembled the daughter grown as full and beautiful as the hedge, a woman who wore the handkerchief and dress that had so long been ignored in the chest.

The woman walked from the fire toward the sleeping parents.

In their sleep, they drew closer together.

The woman didn't speak, but she smiled down on them and raised her right hand in a sweeping motion through the air. When she moved her hand, the darkness dimmed and light filled the little room. As the light began to grow, the walls—with pictures the mother had drawn and with the musket the father kept beside the door—slowly went away. Soon, the light filled the yard and made the flowers and the hedge brighten.

The parents, though still asleep, could hear the sound of the little girl's song from the air itself.

And the song and the light revealed that the mother's chest—so long hidden away in the attic —was in the garden beside the hedge. Little dolls began to dance toward it in time to the music.

Though sleeping and facing the fire and hugging one another, the parents somehow saw all this and were very happy. They hummed the little song in harmony.

But the woman from the fire then raised her left hand and swept it through the air just as she had done with her right hand, and slowly the chest and the garden and the dolls grew dark and disappeared.

The cottage walls came back, and the pictures on the walls and the musket appeared.

The parents let go of each other's hands and their heads began to shake like those of people saying no.

The woman drifted back toward the fire and stood above it for a moment.

She seemed sad as she dwindled back into the flames.

The logs sputtered and the firelight went down and then went out.

The mother and father shivered. They woke up.

When the father opened his eyes, he thought of how his hedge looked.

When the mother opened her eyes, she remembered something in the chest she hadn't seen for years.

They both knew they'd been dreaming, but

couldn't recall exactly what they'd dreamed.

"I need to trim the hedge," the father thought.

"I need to look in the chest," the mother thought.

The next morning, the parents were busy at their chores. The mother was in the kitchen ironing her mother's dress, and the father was turning the soil around the hedge to make it healthier. At exactly the same time, the parents happened to look up.

The mother stared through the window and the father turned around and they both saw their daughter radiant in the sunlight singing a song to a doll that—in the beautiful light of where they were —looked like the child she would someday have.

Without knowing how they knew, the parents began to sing the song.

Listen, you can almost hear it. Even though this story happened long ago in a place so very far away, you can hear the song where you are sitting.